For Vic Contoski
a fine poet and ingenious
            translator

            Nathan Whiting

TRANSITIONS

Books by Nathan Whiting

WHILE COURTING THE SERGEANT'S DAUGHTER

BUFFALO POEM

RANSITIONS

position

and direction

undefined

SEVEN WOODS PRESS

NEW YORK

1972

Seven Woods Press books are published by George Koppelman. For information direct inquiries to:

Seven Woods Press
Post Office Box 32, Village Station
New York, New York 10014

TRANSITIONS

PART 1

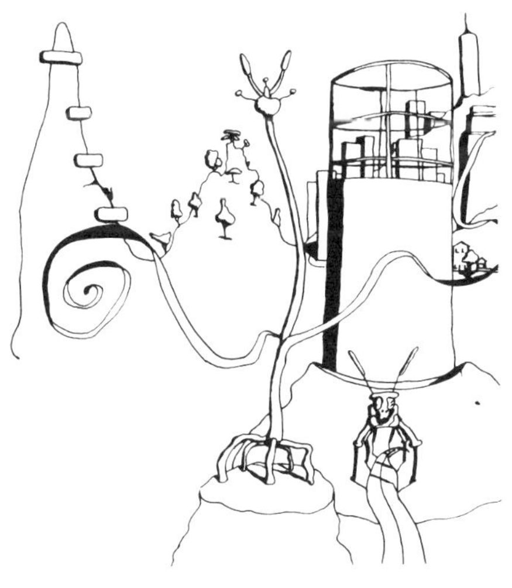

1. There is a real outer world which exists independently of our act of knowing.
2. The real outer world is not directly knowable.

Max Planck, Where is Science Going?

An event in the lives of the Kurelu is known as fast as a boy can run the ditch logs with the news, but no boy is ever sent. . . . The people know the course of things, for the course of things may be thousands of years old, and all they really need to hear is the one word which changes; the event does not. The man's name is called, with the high whoop which relays it onward.

Peter Matthiessen, Under the Mountain Wall

Here they found a Supultian priest, Abbé Piquet, busy at building a fort, and lodging for the present under a shed of bark like an Indian. This enterprising father, ostensibly a missionary, was in reality a zealous political agent, bent on winning over the red allies of the English, retrieving French prestige, and restoring French trade. Thus far he had attracted but two Iroquois to his establishment; and these he lent to Aleron.

Francis Parkman, Montcalm and Wolfe

Carpeted doorways stroke endlessly
the sleeping cat.
This is a land without any tree
in the background.
The soil is recently plowed black
over the used stubble.
No wind, no clouds;
but the haze
is an unlikely result
of bad weather elsewhere.
The erosion is the dust
pushed against each wire fence.
No grass is left anywhere;
as if everything had been burned
and staked out for identification.
A land so fertile
as to be removed of every detail;
unused for beauty.
The soil apologizes for each hill
with blackness.
The houses are so rare
that all life seems to have gone
with the tornadoes,
except one slow tractor
that cancels the last greenness
as if the assembly line moved
and the product stood still.
Each dream fails to change man's size
by making him into a seed
with one solution:
placed into the earth,
a motion
like breath in empty lungs.

This house is a windstorm
built for me
to balance her hair in the chambers
and erase her features.
The landscape is no more
than gravel retched
from a migrating gizzard
with no body.
It is her toe mark.
The grasshoppers are her nostrils,
the leaves her belly,
her belly the face.
She is this way.

There is a tree we sit under,
my arm on her branch.
The birds are so rare
that each insect has lost the fear
against landing on my fingers.
I sit on hollow obsidian
that could be the bone
my skull balances on.
I fight age with hunger
and starve from it
in her presence.
I enter her world:
a windstorm built
to balance my hair in the chamber,
to erase my features
stone against stone
into sand mistaken for dust
in the teeth of an ant.

The lights wait to be put out
by the croaking frog's razor silent eyelash.
But no eyelash
except the grasses reflected
as shadows by water.

Worse when it's winter
and ice captures the grass
in a shallow glaciation
that reaches from hill to hill.
From one I listen for the snow
to extinguish the hundred some distant lights,
so vast as to be a town and forty farms
and the cold drifting
barbed wire.
Each clothesline is an empty eyelash.
Each long eared owl
uses its slow quiet flight
like a frog hidden under the ice in mud,
to survive.
They speak like kittens,
lost in the shape of a tree,
noticing in the moonlight
some motion.
The lights wait to be put out
in the memory.
They never disappear
as completely as what has lived.
The forests have burned.
The grasses have burned without changing,
because they can't
be trampled away
under my defined footprints
and stumbling dog.

Rolicking in the snow,
I speak to the rabbit butchers
before a grove of trees carves me
from the stones I address.
The change is unnoticed.
The white blood
falls from the granite as ice.
The pine tar leaves raise
from the winter a black greenness,
as insincerely as a blizzard.
The butchery of starvation
crawls into a shelter
provided by a tree
for its own stem.
I want to take the snow to be food,
to shit snow,
to press it into ice in my intestines,
to have my final vomit
freeze a thick icicle
from me to the solid earth.
I want my tears to be gall stones
in a stomach that requires to digest
some humble staring creature.

There is a woman in this land.
We speak a language
the characters of which
are the flickerings of a candle on her face.
The sentences are the completeness
that is formed by many zeros.
We are the one before them.
Each tree is a comma
used to separate the billions from the thousands.
I am the resultant,
unable to calculate.

An angel lifts a bag of rice into the temple
carefully separating the taste
from the chewing.
But for me there has been the frustration
of lifting the bags without rest,
without touching the contents.
Sometimes the kind word
is the overused,
the unmeant,
the word spoken by one's self.
Having to write
is to be unable to use
words to pardon myself:
to say: here angel,
I am the rice,
may I have the husk
to press it into paper?
Her answer is at once:
yes take the husk, make paper,
but leave it blank;
and yes make the paper
and praise me on it;
and take the husk,
but don't let me see you;
and no don't make any paper
because what would you do with it;
and no don't take the husk
because taking it would be to you
like taking me.
Each a perception that I don't want any paper.
All refusals.

Tied racers capture each other
and drop as a deer into the snow.
The legs, snagged in each other, snap
with the fall.
The antlers clatter, attracting notice
to an animal self slain.
The puma rests in the guts.
Her teeth, clamped around the heart,
bite down into a bag of red dye
that sends a message through the body
as if it were a nerve.
The cat steps out,
flaps her wings and talons herself to the ground.
Her prey's tawny skin
is blown into the grasslands.
The boulders lift up.
A thousand maggots fly
up the nose and under the fur
so violent are the death throes.

I claim the ears, a hind hoof
and three flank steaks
half rotted away
before I dry them in the sun.
The meat is necessary.
The hoof leads me into the animal's confusion.
I exchange the ears
and hear the terror
that makes each of us run
from the moment
we first listen
until the snags push us together,
pull us apart.
How many? How many?

The man who burns with crushing malice raging, walks
as the spit surrounding his tongue
is lowered by his words.
Wires that hold men together
strain like telephone lines
against the ice storms.
The winter continually breaks its teeth
chewing the calmer winds
as it looses fat to the sun to become brown.
The spring is a useless diarrhea.
The landscape changes under the animals' hooves
and bodies as they are released
from their barns and bred.

The woman I've known
crawls along with the thunderstorms
that move like dark glaciers
over the dustbowl they sodden.
She stands more wet than an eagle
flying up to the ocean's surface.
She wrings her clothing between her palms
that shiver into each other
without once relaxing into fingers.
The leaves try corner by corner
to have their weight blown from under her foot
without her noticing.
The water coming down must go somewhere
when her mouth opens
drinking the air before it becomes mud
fit only for the lungs.
Her clothing becomes the same shape she is,
a shape most bent against the rain.
A calf's throat bawls
an entire rumination from the universe.
The most hopeless leopard
must realize it is just born;
won't come to me.

Her ripples upset the waterspider
who jumps catching the dewdrops
from her trembling arms.
I stand in a waterfall without water,
a stone bowl filled with layers
of more and more
rotted leaves.
She is where the stream now falls
into a clean shallow pool
where the drainage begins.
The mud is washed from her feet
into the distant
debris carrying rivers.
The trees stand as useless as the mountain.
The creatures that live here are small.
Their graves are on the surface
wherever the dead
might become a suburb for maggots.
They grow old in the winter
and thaw out to be warmer in the hot sun
than they were in life.
She shivers
because the air blended with water is cold.
She stands from her own whiteness
that tries to diffuse from her
but fails
with each scattered ripple.
After seeing her use an orange towel,
and dress herself in warmth
equal to her environment,
the trees become green too quickly.
The bark seems uncertain
after hearing her feet.

The face turns
from my face.
I don't know what people mean.
I don't know which face is mine.
It takes more courage than I have
to pick one expression
and intensify,
then use it.

There are bare feet
that have never walked on wooden floors,
but on carpets.
A splinter
or a thorn fallen onto the soft
but cracked earth
is no more risk to the foot
than a glass slipper,
or the tender hide of a calf.
When going barefoot the pain
comes from the rocks,
from the thistles and burrs,
comes from the mud drying on the skin.
The face turns from stepping
on leather too tight for it.
And my face turns
from some thorn
full circle until they meet.
I see that every expression
is made of circles
bending the straight lines
of our tenderest features.

Passing through the lowest doorway
her dry mind is to forget
spinning wool.
All the garments
have been pinched together
by fingers in the imagination.
Every building in a city is a farm house.
But here it's no more
to stand in this room
than to be a sheep in a dark barn.
It is more comfortable to sleep naked
than in wool.

On a table, toward one side,
a candle's beauty is old,
so melted it's hard to tell
what small part still is as it was.
If the first woman dies of childbirth,
the husband's body remains engaging
enough to take another wife.
The woman needs no more than little light.
All day she has woven her veins
and now naked shows her decoration
on her hair covered chest.
The dampness is internal.
The sweat follows them to bed.
The insects don't awaken
after the candle is stopped,
but continue to fill every corner;
only the bedbugs leave.
The lambs pant,
although they are as chewed
as their own pastures
by the clippers that have passed over them.

I don't speak
as the shopkeeper sits tall
and incompletely describes the contents
on his tallest shelf.
All there is is iron,
rusted junk,
weight that bends each shelf down
enough to threaten the next.
What is complete, and depended on,
is the gray wooden ladder
that is used
enough to wear down the steps.
Nothing else is more than a piece of anything;
than an attic
for each incompleted destruction.
He finishes,
and we step over the boxes, gears, engines
and pipes that move their own rust inside
like veins carrying dried hemoglobin.
Each box is like a human cell
with its dry parts
laying heavily on the bottom.
Screws, bolts, nails, fixtures . . .
all sorted as to kind
and no more,
like the residents in a tenement,
like weeds in an arid field
designed for wheat.
I find something I need,
I do, then walk out.
The floor has been softened
but preserved by the pools of oil
that are now one greasyness
under the extremely yellow light bulb.

Reluctantly he is shortened
and tossed into the melting water
by a strong man on his knees begging.
How long are we to enter
and walk out
into a second string heartland?
I've stood in this line
without meaning to
so I could rest for a moment.
A line where the shattered glass
is ruined more by each child
as he passes.
The strong man takes a stone.
The window falls from our heart.
We move to the next line.

Each sidewalk
has its own builder.
The curbs no more meet
than the veins to the arteries.
The clocks have fallen from their towers
and been strapped to each man's wrist,
save the poor
who vacantly stare into each shop
to find out where the sun is.
When the pigeons and the rats become more sterile than man
I'll write poems for those who love on the street.
What drags a mattress onto the street
is sometimes luck,
or death on a mattress.
Or can death keep its mattress
when no one is eager to reach in
and take the ice
from my hepatitic heart.

The briefest wind dries itself
between her lips.
It becomes her hand against mine.
Our fingers hold the shape
as the motion that stays with us,
palms apart,
a slight spreading, an opening.
This is the rhythm that appears in our dreams
without the hands that cause it,
without any sound,
but with the vision a reminder
for the mind.

There is a slightly used color
that I take from the air
as it comes to me.
I ask the buildings to be quiet
as they become rubble
in their own backyards,
and the sun brags
under its resolution.
Red air escapes from the rivers.
The crowded harmonicas
force lips together
in a cruder way than speech.
Our fingers have deafly touched this skin
that is air cooled
by darkness in the evening,
more humid,
more delicately balanced
than the last blade
in a turbine.

Glimpses of terror
like stone pillars are blown
from her forgotten dreams.
Two colors alternate
unequally;
whenever the second comes
it is a personality
used to frighten another one.
I have forgotten her dreams.
I've allowed them to become
a lazy suicide,
or an eventless long wait
to die from a blood poison
dissolving the arteries.
A hope that there is less pain
than from a face exploded by the shotgun
left to rust in my hands.
We are most jealous
of what we've never known,
as if we are birds
having no theories of flight,
or a mystic philosopher
too proud to know himself.
That's one definition of love.
Words are easy to define
because they fail to occur in our lives.
Love: my hand squeezes something
too intricate to understand,
manipulates it without generosity,
but with a precision
that records itself.

The southwind's fire
prepares to clean the insects
from its flames.
The birdseed explodes
from its tight packing.
White grass ribbons
lighter than air are tossed
above the flames in celebration.
In the soil
the roots are like nerves
in the amputated arms
waiting to grow back.
The dry shrubs are torn apart.
All the white is taken from them
like opium in the relaxed lung
of a thousand miles
and one flame.
Among the cinders there are things hurt
and seemingly no more,
but the pain is death throes and starvation
between the heat waves
like steam rising from the rocks.
The slight creek attempts to be water
and no more.
In it the life
that hasn't been choked
by the compressed atmosphere,
is the movement inside coming up
when it has found some coolness
in the air.

Leaves seem to jump
from the ancient countryside,
but are caught by the branches.
The fruit claims its seeds from the ground
and drinks them full of oily juice
before rotting them back
into the shadows
after the bird eggs have also broken
and entered the air.
Leaves in whirlpools
cross the fields and go into a cemetary
containing the best sculpture
in the region:
marble carved by a chisel
making names
that have become too hard to read.
Beside the orchards are houses
so poorly sealed from life
that the dust is swept back
into the roads.
It is August
and the women work as hard
as the field hands.
The dried earth has become so tough
I wonder how
it will be able to freeze solid.
The soil takes the seeds
between its toothpicks
and calls them teeth.
The roots chew their own veins
in the dormancy.

The soft rains cultivate no more
as the heat sealed lungs
fall into the gullies.
The seeds drop
into the flowing dust
and are washed away.
For a tree to grow from this hopeless land
is impossible.
They drag along the death of themselves
and grieve for it
not at all.
For man alone to rebel
is too difficult.
The right hand must complain,
must strike out, reach for
hand open,
and strike again.
The beggars crossing the fields
apologize to me.
The prostitutes
gaze at me without suspicion.
I think that tooth brushing
is to save the teeth from rot,
so I ignore the routine.
I stare into the empty mouths,
and know that from them something grows,
some meagre plant.
I look at the worm holes
in the soil,
and for now, not at man
but to man
from grief.

PART 2

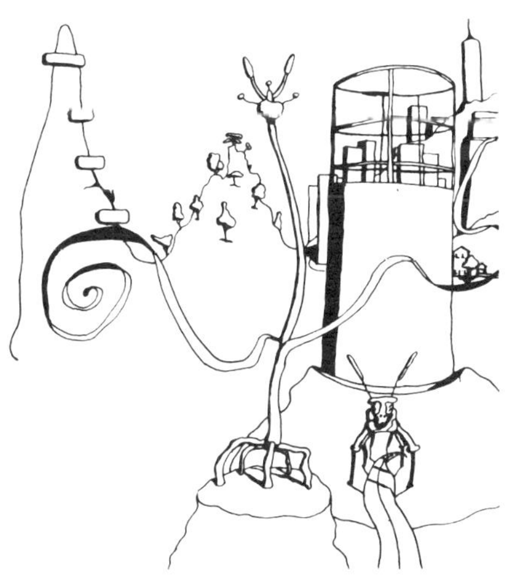

The chain of cause and effect could be quantitatively verified only if the whole universe were considered as a single system—but then physics has vanished, and only a mathematical scheme remains.

Werner Heisenberg,
The Physical Principles of the Quantum Theory

a cry so unearthy and so weird that even the man of stoutest heart will start in affright: a cry that can only be likened to a scream of demoniac laughter. This is the cry of the male Cougar. If it is answered by the female the response will be similar to the wail of a child in terrible pain.

W. A. Perry,
'The cougar', The big game of North America

Asking to be a humbler one than I
you are fed
like a stone is by the earth.
Being a blood crystal,
elegantly shaped and transparent,
you are melted like a fire
evolved from scarlet blossoms of ice.
I would take you in light
that is an apple's fragrance cut open,
or in the dark,
or so near the dark as to hint your face
when you bend back
with your head to smile.
The simplest desert stream
would refuse to be so clear.
Man's most significant garbage heap
would be stretched across the earth
less noticeably.
You ask me to say something
so that I might understand.
It is possible,
I might; but what to be said
is: grass no taller than the dust
will bend to cushion you.
For a moment I deny my role
only for yours.
This bed should be a half dried tobacco leaf
and we no larger than aphids
should use it until it turns white.
And one of us should say:
as your gift seeps from the mountain
and I come up from brown rivers,
you bend as if trapped in snow.

You wash your feet
in water squeezed
from each blind animal you catch.
You take the hand
from each misplaced elbow
and reach it over for mine,
that we might turn somewhat.
Your waist is softer
than I imagined breasts.
With a woman it is comforting to relax
beside the idea that follows her motions.
That I might turn
like that arctic bird
wildly, floating like the lightest cork,
yet to be waterlogged by the great distance.
That I might come to be sand
followed by another wingspread.
That she might choose me
and lengthen her neck
into the air
to be kissed.
Phalaropes fly over the sea;
the sky a certain lavender,
the flower,
the dull waves the stem.
On this land
our recognition
is like a grave
being eroded from a hill
as if to live.

If you were sand to be fused into glass
it would be a slight injury
to perfection.
But there is no furnace
so calm as to do it.
Silk that comes from a perfect seed.
In you it is below the closed eyes,
is the bones
when skin covers them loosely,
in the way that breath covers the smoke
while removing the intoxication.
The crystal is human too,
but so much a tiny part
as to stand in the finger
for half a motion
before it is again dissolved.
Time is what man thinks a crystal is;
but it's not,
for all of us bend
from moment to desire
and the movement to it.
What happens goes by too easily.
So we come together.
When you must leave, there is glass.
Then you are painted in the distance,
as if in a furnace
with lips as tight
as an animal hiding beside a wall
from its own slight body;
is a day
for each of us.

I am an hour
cooling the fire
into a black dawn.
These are desires too certain
to be given up.
I've held the most delicious food
to my face
when I was least hungry,
and it wasn't like this.
You have more man to live with
than me.
The accident that put a child inside you,
became a necessity
to narrow your life into his.
He took each pain
with you in his nervous
uncertain hands.
If I make the same mistake
I will cheat a son
one father.
I'll destroy some mirror
that is silvered on both sides.
How could this man,
that you love also,
understand this concern
as he rests in your absence?
I close my eyes
as if to see you
would cause you so little grace
that you would fall
into his one bent arm
and my armless silence.

Trees planted evenly for two hundred miles
will never bend.
Why do you?
In the more settled hours
a tornado could skip
every structure on earth,
and there would be no more than the sound.
Candles in a chandelier
move as the air does.
The flames are thin drums
playing shadows with their motions.
This way to make compliments
would be saying
what should be obvious in our thoughts.
We search for what is obvious,
demand it,
so we can make it more obscure:
to be human.
This listening is more than a conversation
held between our fingers
wherever they have stopped.
They are restless until the last candle
hardens between them.
My teeth say:
why do your teeth speak
more than their words?
We use our tongues when listening.
We hold our breath
so it will never get farther than our mouths.
If there is this slight skull
behind your skin,
then why are there bones
where the sand meets the first planets?

When no door opens
you seem to move with greater speed
between them
posing for each.
Until at one you find a certain man,
claim him, so he can be accustomed to you.
Who cares if custom says it's the other way?
Which is the more striking,
the male, the female?
The more splendid one
rests on the ground,
and the more speculative one
comes there.
Only to you;
some dream,
and you only to him.
The place where we live is a gatherer
that takes people into forgetfulness.
We are burning calmness, cinders,
the 1.2% octachloro-4.7-methanotetrahydroindane
in the insects' threadlike nerves:
a flicked cigarette.
I feel in your hand
a mere thinness
with a certainty to its motion
that becomes fingers.
The universe is a stairway
and one imagined above it.
Our hands take this step,
reach into our acceptance
and find nothing to refuse between us.
and one imagined above it,
and above that a face
distracted by half nudity
smoking her cigarette.

The distance:
the poles that contain the wires
are tubes buried under the ground.
The clotheslines are tubes
buried under the ground,
in someone's attempt
to disturb the geology.
The quarries are building excavations.
The landscape is shoveled
from hole to hole.
We meet
between the distance.
The bricks are scraped together
enough to build houses.
You come less from a place
than from an attitude.
There is nothing to be seen
from any window you have
that can be connected with a person
I know.
You identify yourself by the clothes you've made
and the bargains
you have purchased.
I want to lie to myself about your age,
to treat you like you were eighteen,
so I can be eighteen.
How can there be any sense of what we are
without locations?
You carefully guard your origins
by forgetting the places
so you can separate
your involvement
from the poles that contain the wires.

You've picked yourself for silence
the ocean where the rocks are shined
into still hot magma in a slag heap.
You must think water is the kind of dust
that makes dust less polished.
You place your hands into the water
to pull sand from between the rocks
as if you could use it
to be less naked.
In tapered gloves
your fingers would seem smaller.
That would be a calmness.
Beside an oxygen furnace
you could at least see the silence
in the steel as it's poured out;
never mind the energy behind it.
You could watch the smoke curl away
as if it wanted to be a tornado,
before the it
in the thing is blown away.

We are together,
but I count the fencepoles in an empty field
for silence.
Then I quit,
for there is no such field.
There is instead you
in this city
where the fences are built between roofs
as if to say:
this rain is mine
that yours.

Lost among the cobblestones
there is a dropped grape
pressed into wine by the slow rainfall.
You shop beside something
just in from the harbor
that has every texture
in its single color.
There is an empty shape
designed into the warehouses
that make the street seem dead end
when it's not.
A street used by a few vendors
who squat beside their vegetables,
and for us to come.

You are a lonely marketer
fingering the melons and searching
for the movement
that might interrupt my shadow.
This wet street,
with people crouched for dryness
between the flies,
marks the footprints,
then erases them.
The umbrellas touch all the air that moves.
Perhaps you haven't noticed yet,
but they are involved
with our meeting.
You are a certain grayness
worn into the color
you've smeared onto your face.
You are on the pavement most sunlit.
I walk over to its hardness.

The first thing
when the woods has been manufactured
so there are no animal tracks,
is it will have just snowed.
The mirrors will have become slabs
for you to stand in front of.
We begin our conversation
with weather reports meant to be words
to test our voices.
We slowly walk barefoot in the snow
as we leave the first footprints in it.
The air is no longer able to keep warm.
It comes to our nakedness,
but has no arms,
so it can only fall dead
to the ground.
That's how distant we are
from what we touch.
I reach down to pick some flower
that has been frozen into a dry seed pod.
I offer it to you.
It's the flower
that has caused the wind
to form a canyon in the snow.
A canyon so small
that your foot covers it.
The spine, as it sinks into your back,
may be longer and turns away
more easily.
Our ankles melt bracelets of snow
as I offer you this weed:
as I would hand you a cigarette
if it could take long enough
to whisper the reason.

Around us is the inertia
drying the water into humidity.
It is difficult to wet my lips
between the bones
that surround my teeth.
Where we have come to talk
there is a pressure that has chipped the rocks
and leaves into dust.
But it's easier to stare
into our imaginations.
Each forgets to tell the other one
what we have come here for.
At times we are each a tree
carefully planted into the whitewalled mouth
of a tire.
At times I am the orphanage
in your womb.
At times our words
are trained animals
sneaking out of the forests.

I haven't used a thousand miles
to build a single wall,
or to describe each tree I found here,
and how nearly the weeds
come to covering the barbed wire.
It is a marsh
with one river through it.
The heavy mud is dust.
You are held in the air
by mosquitos that will never bite
because they pull strings
that a gypsy moth larva
walked from a tree to the ground on.

The whirlwind stirring the ocean
breathes in
before calling itself tremendous.
So what does it mean
to continually fill our lungs
to keep the air as fresh as it should be
in the same way that a good bartender
keeps a glass filled
when you least notice it?
We could drink together
and separate all there is
between I and you.
Or drink ourselves into sleep,
not caring who we are
or why we are together
or who we have left alone.
But we shouldn't drink
because there is something else
that has brought us here.
We have argued philosophy
for the pleasure of a draw.
Neither one of us is so confident
as to be anything more than he wishes for.
There is what you see
and describe.
Then I must tell you this one thing:
the defects worn into the earth
are called perfection
by the sweat on your belly,
by two olive trees
sharing one root
and two fields,
and by the wheat below
that rattles to the distance
to be seen.

A clown with two legs
would sit as quietly,
with one smile painted,
and then smile into it.
There is no pretense
in the role when it becomes absurd enough.
The comedy is to be together
as we search the floor
for some motion where a cockroach
has startled us,
and then stomp on it.
The laughter is half nervous,
but the painted exaggerations
that surround it
are very careful and certain.
There is no animal that paints his face
to imitate himself
as we do.
We perform to survive,
because we have entered our camouflage
to search for each other.
We hide ourselves most of the places we go,
no matter what clothing we use
to change our outsides.
But there are times
when you come to me
and lay back with the night
as your only disguise.
Your thought is to sit beside a mountain
sculpted into man,
and retreat into the molten isolation
of some prairie.

In this darkness
the light becomes what the shadow
reversed it to be.
We deal with the night's problems
by inventing nouns
to request the presence
that may help some tiny fear,
some instability.
The narrowness at your waist
has a brass chain over dark cloth
that I pull
as if it were a ring in your eyelash
that would cause you to sleep.
Some nervousness comes instead,
like two birds having no more room for courtship
than a high wire in the wind.
If a kiss could slice a face in two,
or a quiet rainfall burst open a tree;
then the eye that opens
struggles slightly to be so.
Or changes its mind
and opens easily,
drawing away
as best it can.
Then, while time is longer than this poem
and shorter than the first three lines,
we feel what can be seen between us.
It is the dust
that creates one shadow
in the lace curtains beyond the branches
they are twisted from.

If we repeat every action of the night
backwards, together,
the sheets will become
more wrinkled.
That's why some men lie on stone:
it is flat and constant,
it doesn't sag in the middle.
Now we come to the one way
to be in two dreams at once:
that is to sleep in one
while you have the other.
You might sleep
in the leaves that grow on branches
no taller than you are
when lying down.

Or naked on grass
burned flat against the dirt
that is rain covered
where the erosion begins as streams
leading to two great rivers
lost beyond the gullies.
Your sheets could be the blowing ashes
as they are brought to the ground
by the moisture each morning.
No distance greater than a fog
could make you conspicuous,
or change my coming to you.
But were you to stand in the middle
of a crowded room,
I would still meet you.
I would ask you if anyplace you knew
meant anything.
If you said no,
I would say: where do you dream from?

A cat can walk up nonexistent stairs
and not come down.
I take your blouse button by button
until it unfolds.
I have touched the willingness, the acceptance,
the invitation
as much as I've touched the cloth.
Now it is device after device
that man has engineered a woman
into her clothes with,
until we get to the woman.
We each have ribs that can be seen
as we breathe.
I move an arm to change the way
we are placed together
so that we may share an expression.
There is a way it happens:
I'm aloof, you're ostensive.
Your movements call my aloofness something
that makes it something else.
The light we are in is too gentle
for you to have the slightest pretense,
or to grin nervously
and not mean it.
You love me, see me this way.
We share faith
and call it joy between words.
Such as adorable,
an easy word and out of style,
but you have used it,
your eyes like a child
that has known pregnancy.

Your being here
is a movement with great motion
resembling, just then, rest.
We are together so little
it has to be both,
there is no time for repetition.
Today we want to say the obvious,
but avoid saying it
because we don't want to.
If I were the man and you the woman—
is what we mean as we express it.

If the light is dim enough,
it will burn between the shadows.
Imagine a candle
that moves around us in a circle;
that the furniture casts long, exact shadows
that we have to move through
to meet each other.
Then I would believe in astrology:
that the signs are the furniture,
the sign of the table, the chair, the bookcase . . .
Then I would read my charts in the corner
and live by them.
But to meet we ride subways.
The stars are meaningless.
We live in the heart, in the vein
of a shadow.
Its charts are the rumble
as the uptowns pass through the stations.
The obvious is that we hug or kiss
or make love.
The other thing is
that those born between the shadows
become trees that are just a whisp
in the lightning.

PART 3

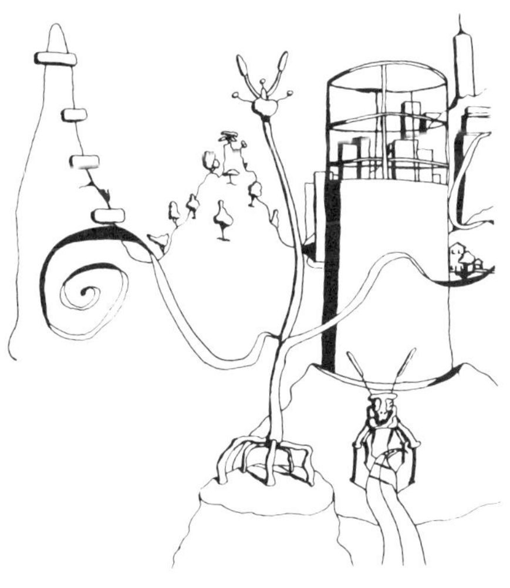

... the particles may be anywhere. Though energy and momentum are conserved, we cannot say *where* and *when* this conservation is realized, so to this extent the space-time description eludes us. The other extreme case occurs when the space-time positions of the two particles are accurately determined. The momenta and the energies are then uncertain, and rigorous conservation cannot be asserted. When we recall that the conservation laws for particles are special examples of causal relations for individual processes, we see that the foregoing illustrations exhibit the incompatibility between strict causality and an accurate space time description.

A. d'Abro, *The Rise of the New Physics*

Searchers found footprints of this human victim which were easily followed in the sandy, gravelly formation that led to a waterhole where he had, before being attacked by the puma, quenched his thirst, washed his wounds, used a small piece of his clothing for a bandage, and then scribbled his name on a 'rock in his own blood'.

Stanley P. Young & Edward Goldman,
The Puma: Mysterious American Cat

In the story of the continual creation of soil under us, the desert is the silent preface.

Peter Farb, *Living Earth*

A light infinity.
A river,
and below that another world:
the red stone that is gouged into pipes
and smoked dry.
On the walls there should be flowerpots
watered by defrosting refrigerators.
Watered by rivers
that are heatwaves without banks.

How easily I say this.
How easily I make it meaningless.
The earth doesn't say a volcano,
but utters five shrubs that grow together
in the prairie beside it.
All the harmonics of a body in motion
are waiting for me to look away from vision.
For Nathan Whiting to write a poem
is a waste of the hours
he could spend in a foundry stoned on noise.
Who could imagine a hell
with mad houses and hard beds?
Instead it is sandstone
that burns with no direction for the flames to rise to.
What if the mad were cured
and made into great flame arches in the sky?
What if the damned were to become water,
and after a million years of being steam,
learned how to flow?
The rusty sandstone we smoke
is the vapor, the ash Sometimes everything
present in the world is smoke.
Gray in color
is still gray in color.

Bricks remain soft
where eagles share the furnace with them.
I plant a desert
so the snow may never hide the mice from the eagles.
Grass should be the only foothills,
where a breath
looks like snow disappearing into the himalayas.
One flake, to be so close,
it must be an eagle.
He goes from tree to tree
where there are no trees,
like a rabbit without holes
would have to be born under the leaves
in the most shadow.
The clouds are an earth.
They are too green to have flowered,
too white to have accepted the rain
as their own roots.
Two eagles. Their landing
is as sudden as two swifts
flying through a hole large enough for one.
The eagles fall into the dust
and come up holding stones in their talons
to stuff into their gizzards.
The creatures that live under the stones
are small and held together
as if the water inside them were glue.
Why else would the springtails
crawl so deeply into their holes
to avoid the daylight?
The mountains are feathers shed by eagles.
Destroy the world with feathers.

Shadows come from the lava
and walk into the man
to warm his breath.
We find ourselves without evidence.
Above, a great bear
hangs from his tree asleep.
He makes us so nervous
that we build fires
and pile stones over our coffins
so we can feel safe to die.
Spiders make bridges
higher than we can see the ground from.
They tell the blind everything
through the poison in their mandibles,
and horrify the deaf
by weaving lightning into the clouds.

I walk behind and away from the mountains
into the haze called foothills.
The ground is bare
because rocks have fallen
under the trees and the trees
have become dry firewood
against the late summer
of some year without eagles.
I live among creatures
able to walk where there is no light,
able to step on ice cubes
suspended from the sky,
able to hunt butterflies by screaming at them,
able to dodge the stones
in the ground they move through,
and slice the death from a fly
at eight feet with their tongues.

The elephants wander everywhere
making footprints in the trees
with their trunks.
The sultans grab boulders
and use modern equipment to crush them
into polish for sand storms
tasted by the famines.
In the great hearths,
where sorcerers can sing as loudly
as they can remain invisible,
the glassworker has made his sweat
into pollen on the flowers
he has nearly made perfect.
He never sees them as being false.
Gardens have been made into front rooms
where great sultans stare into their drinks
and smell the dinners
prepared in forty towers.
The quietly tinkling flowerpetals
make music against the walls
that open here and there
into elevators.
Wings have gone to the powerlines.
Eyes hover near diamonds
buried in the rivers.
From the snow comes precious gems
that can never be mined
because they are turquoise and thunderstone
that become shadows in the pitchforks.
What other gardens can there be
now that there is glass?
The walls collapse.
Beautiful.

Beautiful indeed,
but written about
before photographed by a thousand amateurs
who made the image into a black postage stamp.
We explore the planets
to find the coldest people in the universe,
so those freezing on earth
can have fur woven from methane snowflakes.
To climb a dead 90,000 foot mountain
is to prove there is a god on Jupiter.
The rings are ocean bottoms in the sky.
Nowhere do they slip into notice
in less than 40,000,000,000 years.
The sand is lighter.
The mountains become solid.
These opposite forces whisper to each other
as they wait.
I will be the first man to climb the mountain
a mile shorter
than the other one.
But not the first: a dream
of being close enough to see the greatness
as the bare shadow it is.
I imagine it is a woman come to me
clothed in the snow that has always blown there.
Two mountains are shoved together
at the base and lifted
to peaks that let all but the hardness be eroded.
I choose isolation.
Across the softest valleys the mountains are green clay.
Temples of quarried jade.

A mermaid in the mountain air
has wings for a fishtail.
Her feathers loosen
and float into the gorges
from her rock
that is a carpeting of hard cloud.
She holds her fingers together
hoping that no silver can be found in the bedrock,
that no trees will cover the slopes,
that no pastures
or wild game will come near her,
and that the snow will be too dangerous for skiing;
so she can be alone
when she grows old
and too ugly to look at.
The talus is the first snowfall,
the blue veins in a pregnancy.
Visible when she is naked is her chin.
That is all anyone has ever seen of her.
She draws her legs together
and uses her hair and her breasts
for warmth.
The mountain goats think her fair skin is black.
The food will no longer be brought to her
by the ants.
She huddles against the rock
and begs it to be a volcano.
The snow buries the tracks of the vultures
who have hunted her for centuries
and now believe her immortal.
The wolves come
to sleep with her for warmth.
She knows they will tear her to pieces
in ten days when she bleeds.

The weight we carry away,
as we clean our hiding places,
has bent us and made it easier to hide.
The eagles sour the canyons
and the vultures remove the suicides.
This wind has made monuments from the rock
for each of them to live on.
Our shapes stumble from the cliffs
into·the canyons
and are shattered before the fall is over.
To hide we must never move when it happens,
never allow our trail
to come up to us.

The vultures must wonder
at the animals they never hunt
and think them gods.
They sit stinking in hunger
beside great rivers where the bear fish.
They look down into the water,
where they have no god,
and grunt at the ripples.
Man is carrion.
The vultures grind their own rocks
to build landmarks with our bones.
These are temples
the dead would make from the roots entering their graves,
but there are no souls to do it.
The earth is cut into slabs
and hung in the canyons
to dry.
The vultures come with gold
to make every detail
resemble the animals they saw hunted,
as they waited in awe.

The men are fighting this war
so temporary they can remember
what dry sheets can do
for undressing.
There are no more graveyards.
I walk a corpse to the bricks
that crumble in the mortar.
I walk him home in the night
beside the same trees
and over the same gravel
that's marked by some whore's feet
as she walks for the wounded.
Walls with holes cut for the woodwork
use up the forests as quickly
as the refugees can chop firewood.
There are no houses for the young men
who have left their shadows standing
long after they have fallen
in the spring battles.
Vulture nests are needed in the branches,
for once, very needed.

Here stood a man at the point of dying,
deciding for a moment
which way to fall,
and for once taking the least gallant way,
as there was no risk.
The mountains gave their own light.
There were no stars.
The ranges were like cradles and breasts.
If there weren't any rocks,
then the trees could grow
so that in the bark everything happening in life
could be recorded.
Then to strike the ground so hard
there is nothing.

The earth was once a thousand feet above us.
The giant creatures
have worn the rest into oceans.
You can see in the hills
streaks from their blood.
Mountains have eroded from their gall stones.
Their eyes have melted,
in fires they pulled down from the sun,
and became lakes with blue waves
moving backwards in the wind.
Their death masks are needles
splintered from the cliffs.

Could gravel?
Could gravel with blood spilled on it
while still in the gizzard,
somehow not become sand?
In the fires I burn on the gravel,
the pieces are flattened like lead.
I imagine a dinosaur enduring a skunk
swallowed whole by surprise.
My bones become sand.
They are bleached sticks
that make the leaves hold together
against the insects.
They grow where the stone goes down forever
into the earth.
You think you have seen something
in the mountains that come above the ground,
but it's a little thing
placed so high as to make it hard
for the trees to be the tallest windbreaks
in the world.
The ranges are skulls turned to sinterstone
that all tales are written on.

I am a bird with no dust in my gizzard.
I walk with the flat prairies to be to my imagination
what the spartan grass is to my memory:
the mildew in a steer's mouth.
I repeat the motions
needed to come from the shell
that has grown me.
The smaller the cupboards,
the more comfortable the nests
I build in them.
The night is dark.
Candles are dangerous.
Electricity is no more than the wires
that go through a land where orchards
are without ladders
that can be reached by the nighthawk.

Man is carrion,
and after he dies his work is carrion, also.
His livestock is the grasshopper.
When he fights the birds
it's because he's grown so hungry
he must eat his livestock.
He waits for us to fly down
to eat his grasshoppers,
so he can kill us because he is hungry.
He looks up, for there are male birds
that prance in the mountains
400 miles to the distance.
At the mountain's base
trees are broken.
Man thought the mountains were moving.
He thought he could move faster than the ranges.
And he thought
no drought would be enough to fry the grasshoppers.

I have liked people
who are less intelligent
than most people I know.
I find beauty in birds
that fly clumsily in the smog.
I like poetry worse
than my own,
but it can't be found
and it is everywhere.
So I go to the top of the very important mountains
and use the snow blowing away
to hide in.
I become a spirit
stealing from those hiding in the valley
who have food to eat.
I see the sunrise sooner
and shout to wake up the roosters.
I see that what makes one mountain range
seem like a wall to another
is a force as invisible
as the greatest we can define.
A hurricane pulls the sea onto the land.
A tornado lifts handfuls of dust
into a half destroyed city.
Clouds can fall below the peaks
where the roosts are too high for birds.
They are black rocks
that stand above the snow line.
I could ski once and go so far that the hounds sent after me
would think I was a dead man.
In the morning the tallest rocks
are snow covered.
The world has become a lake
with ripples moving more slowly
than ice crushed into steel.

On the cliffs there are amphitheaters
so high no one could play to them,
so steep no one would dare act in them.
They are built of pottery
so soft that grass could slice them,
if any grass could grow there.
They are named
so that each nymph hiding in the crevaces
will feel it is for her.
What can be seen from the seats
are reptiles
too nearsighted to see farther then the edges
of their cracks
before seeming afraid.
Walk to them if you can find the way.
Become lost among the insects
that hide in the rocks.
Become a shape like time
that can move above the cliffs
and keep from falling.
Come to one needle so high
that legends have been made from below.
Jump as if you had wings for skis
in the fog that snows forever
on the plucked dove horizon.
A hundred suns would make more light
than our bodies could freeze in.
See the trees as firewood
and hold on to them
and drag them with you.
Land where the flowers become pollen
too heavy to reach
the blossom next up the mountain.

Above the canyons
flowers drift toward the water
more rarely than stone splinters down from the walls.
This is the harshness
we have come here for.
Inside the canyons
tiny birds live
by feeding on pollen
as it falls over the rims.
These birds are too small to be seen by the grasshoppers
that jump past
not realizing what they are falling into.
From that point on
it's impossibly steep,
and everything leading into the earth
is impossibly steep.
The cliffs form their own organs.
None are lungs.
They can call themselves nothing.
The chasm between the cliff walls
needs creatures to live in it,
to hear the breath that was never asked for.
Someday the water will enter.
The walls will have no more need to stand.
The turtles will find mud flats,
when before they had no way to rest
because the currents
could move their size to the ocean.
Never before has the sand become mud enough
to start a river,
and to hold animals in the traps
set to hold the feet that pass over.

When sulphur had left the monster's nose,
and the white in his eyes sailed by,
I made from his tail
a great pipe;
and it was very hard to do.
The sand and the mountains met
with their heads bent back
and faults open.
The monster tried to steal the land
because he loved to make deserts
to drag down the maidens
from the stars into.
Crawling over the leaves,
the ants called the earth a nightfall
and followed the same tunnels
we use in daylight.
So from his ears I made radar screens
and they were very clear.
When I stared into the crystal balls
I found among his gallstones,
his footprints formed
and he came back.
The ants slipped down from between the boulders
and built their homes.
Cold air fell from the monster's nose
into mists that covered the bare trees.
The valleys seemed to be candlewax
as each detail fell with the pollen grains
into the crevaces.
There was a god that created night
to test his lightning in.
No creature had slept on harder beds,
or looked at his striking face
in clearer or more rapidly vanishing mirrors.

They stepped from the solid rock
and I knew they couldn't be one of us.
These were children come to the wilderness
to cry from their caves in the wind.
Their playbox was red sandstone,
not washed, but chipped
and burned in the crevaces.
Here the animals are dried
and seeds are placed in their footprints.
The rocks are as bright
as a plant's shadow.
The seeds are the unfinished boulders
that melt from the orifices.
The children are tired.
Placed in their minds is the fading away
to where flutes hang in the sky
without form,
where they can climb without spider webs
to blow them.
The children find precious reasons
to take down carefully
because there are things too light
to be sandstone.
They are weaker than the joy
of throwing cliffs against each other.
They pick targets.
They grab lizards and squeeze them,
as our children do plastic toys.
The lizards have no voices,
but dart their tongues out
to catch flies to do the screaming instead.
There are no flies on the children.

Somewhere else, deeper in our skins,
the coldness blows ice
onto the rocks to make powder.
The last beautiful woman's kind remains
takes that powder in her hands
and washes her face with it.
A plant, green enough
to make one imagine the color blue,
is crushed to make perfume.
What could be said to make the desire stay,
when but to see her
is something bitter
until she has touched you.
Striking enough to rise above the shadows
and be white,
the moon is as close in this near daylight
as the breast of a woman pregnant
for a thousand generations
dressed in cotton.
A silken woman
weaves a child from her breast.
Somehow, when she is in the water,
a snowfall is powerful
and freezes her like a distortion.
I forget I am a child forever to be born,
and that the moon is a ridge
to fall away into nothing
with each touch from the tides.
Look at her face.
Once in a thousand tries it's an expression
when it is motionless.
Then desire confuses the would be suicides.
They want not a woman,
but children.

The hairs covering the sex of the earth
are too thin.
Blister beetles have fallen
on the flowers that bloom on ledges
that will sheer onto the sandstone
spread below.
The mole and the tame pig will eventually meet.
The differences between them
drink from the same bottles.
The smoke clouds hang pale in the bottomlands.
We go down into the storerooms
that are filled with the pollen of the rope plant.
I return flair filled.
A kind, delicate wasp is stung
into places where the television reception
is so good there are no aerials.
The birds have to land naked
on the bridges.
I am a flower. My petals
are venetian blinds.
Each day I open the petals to live without shadow.
A tree a hundred years old
could fall and be silent,
petrify into sand on a discarded golf course.
Sweatstone is to be found
and dragged off to make incense
melted in the heat of lilac grass
and hay flowers that have grown dry
under the sun's silicosis.
In the valley is the rock I have taken you to
called the ocean.
To our ankles we stand in it.
We never chose to have water be our blood.

Books From Seven Woods Press

SUSAN FROMBERG SCHAEFFER, The Witch and
the Weather Report

NATHAN WHITING, *Transitions*

Cover drawing by Nathan Whiting.

Designed and printed by the Profile Press of New York